DATE DUE			

A Picture Book of

WILD ANIMALS

Written by Joanne Gise
Illustrated by Roseanna Pistolesi

Troll Associates

Library of Congress Cataloging-in-Publication Data

Gise, Joanne.
 A picture book of wild animals / by Joanne Gise; illustrated by
Roseanna Pistolesi.
  p.   cm.
 Summary: Brief text and illustrations introduce twelve wild
animals including the giraffe, zebra, and American buffalo.
 ISBN 0-8167-1908-X (lib. bdg.)   ISBN 0-8167-1909-8 (pbk.)
 1. Zoology—Africa—Juvenile literature. 2. Animals—Juvenile
literature. [1. Zoology—Africa. 2. Animals.] I. Pistolesi,
Roseanna, ill. II. Title.
QL336.G57 1990
599—dc20   89-37334

LION

It's easy to tell a male lion from a female lion. The male has long, thick hair growing over his head, neck, and shoulders. This hair is called a *mane*. It protects the lion when he is fighting.

Adult males and females live with their *cubs*, or young, in groups called *prides*. When the male cubs are about two years old, the adult males chase them away. Then the younger males form their own prides.

The females, called *lionesses*, hunt large animals like zebra and antelope. They use their sharp teeth and claws to kill their prey. Even though the lionesses do most of the hunting, the male lions get to eat first.

GIRAFFE

The giraffe's six-and-a-half-foot-long neck lets it eat tasty leaves that grow high in the trees. Its long neck has only seven bones. That's the same number of bones in your neck. But a giraffe's bones are much bigger than yours.

Its neck isn't the only part of a giraffe that is big. Its legs are about six feet long. They help make the giraffe the tallest animal in the world—between fourteen and eighteen feet tall!

A giraffe usually runs away from trouble. But if a lion attacks it—watch out! The giraffe will kick the lion with its feet.

ELEPHANT

An elephant's trunk is its nose, arm, and hand. Sniffing the air, an elephant can smell an enemy miles away. Small, fingerlike bumps on the end of its trunk let an elephant pick up objects as small as a berry. Elephants also use their trunk to spray water over themselves and make loud trumpeting noises.

An elephant is the largest land animal. It can weigh up to 14,000 pounds. Its thick skin alone weighs about 2,000 pounds!

Elephant families live in large herds. Baby elephants stay with their mothers until they are ten to fourteen years old. Then they start their own families. An elephant can live to be sixty years old.

VERVET MONKEY

Swinging through the trees, a vervet monkey looks for leaves, fruit, and insects to eat. Its long tail helps the monkey keep its balance as it runs and jumps.

Vervets, like all monkeys, live in groups. They like to be with one another. Very often, monkeys will groom each other. This is a sign of friendship. It also cleans the monkeys and gets rid of insects that bother them.

ZEBRA

No two zebras are striped the same way. Their stripes may make the animal look funny. But they help the zebra hide from its enemies by making it hard to see.

Zebras run across the grassy plains in herds. Each herd is led by a male, or *stallion*. A herd also has several *mares*, or females, and their young, called *foals.* Young stallions live in their own herds until they are strong enough to take over a herd from another male zebra.

Lions like to eat zebras. When a lion attacks it, the zebra bites, and kicks with its sharp hooves.

CHEETAH

A cheetah runs faster than any other animal. It hunts antelope and gazelle. The cheetah slips quietly through the long grass until it is near its prey. Then it leaps up and runs as fast as seventy miles an hour. But the cheetah can only run this fast for a short distance. If its prey can stay ahead of it, the cheetah will soon get tired and find something else to chase.

Cats can pull in, or *sheathe*, their claws, but the cheetah cannot. Its claws are out all the time. This helps it kill its prey quickly.

HIPPOPOTAMUS

At night, hippos walk around, eating grass and shrubs. But during the day, hippos stay in the water. They are very good swimmers and can stay underwater for up to six minutes at a time. They also like to lie in the mud.

If a hippo does not stay wet, its skin will dry out and the hippo will die. Baby hippos are even born underwater! While in the water, they often lie on their mothers' backs, safe from hungry crocodiles.

GORILLA

Baby gorillas ride around on their mothers' backs. If their mothers didn't carry them, the young gorillas would not be able to keep up with the adults in the search for food. Baby gorillas stay with their mothers until they are about six years old.

Gorillas live in family groups called *troops*. The oldest male is the head of the family. He is called a *silverback*. This is because the hair on a gorilla's back turns gray as he gets older.

SPOTTED HYENA

For many years, people thought that hyenas only ate what was left of other animals' kills. Animals who do this are called *scavengers*. But when some scientists watched hyenas at night, they discovered a surprising thing. A pack of hyenas will chase and kill prey such as zebras and other large animals. Hyenas will even chase lions away from their kills.

Some people think that hyenas laugh, but this is not true. When a hyena is excited, it makes a shrill cry that sounds like laughter.

IMPALA

If a herd of impala sees a lion or a cheetah, they quickly leap away. An impala can run as fast as fifty miles an hour and can jump thirty feet. They will even jump over each other's backs. This helps the impala get away from danger. It also confuses the animal that is chasing them.

Some impala herds are called *harem herds*. They are made up of females and their young, plus one male who is the leader. Males who are not strong enough to lead a harem herd stay together in *bachelor herds* or live alone. Sometimes two males fight. They hit each other with their long, curved horns. The winner will be the leader of the harem.

WHITE RHINOCEROS

A rhino's horns are not made of bone. They are made of hair! But the hair is so hard and thick that it is as strong as bone.

The only land animal that is bigger than a white rhino is the elephant. A white rhino can be up to six feet tall and fifteen feet long. It weighs about 7,000 pounds. Its heavy skin is two inches thick. When it isn't eating grass, a rhino likes to lie in water or mud. This keeps it cool and protects it from the hot sun.

Rhinos can't see well at all. They often charge at other animals—and miss!

AFRICAN BUFFALO

The African buffalo is probably the most dangerous land animal. It has a very bad temper and sometimes attacks for no reason. With its strong body, heavy hooves, and horns that spread four feet wide, this buffalo can even kill a lion!